Notes for adults

TADPOLES NURSERY RHYMES are structured to provide support for newly independent readers. The books may also be used by adults for sharing with young children.

The language of nursery rhymes is often already familiar to an emergent reader, so the opportunity to see these rhymes in print gives a highly supportive early reading experience. The alternative rhymes extend this reading experience further, and encourage children to play with language and try out their own rhymes.

If you are reading this book with a child, here are a few suggestions:

1. Make reading fun! Choose a time to read when you and the child are relaxed and have time to share the story.

2. Recite the nursery rhyme together before you start reading. What might the alternative rhyme be about? Why might the child like it?

3. Encourage the child to reread the rhyme, and to retell it in their own words, using the illustrations to remind them what has happened.

4. Point out together the rhyming words when the whole rhymes are repeated on pages 12 and 22 (developing phonological awareness will help with decoding language) and encourage the child to make up their own alternative rhymes.

5. Give praise! Remember that small mistakes need not always be corrected.

First published in 2008 by
Franklin Watts
338 Euston Road
London NW1 3BH

Franklin Watts Australia
Level 17/207 Kent Street
Sydney NSW 2000

Text (Humpty Dumpty at Sea)
© Brian Moses 2008
Illustration © Jan Lewis 2008

The rights of Brian Moses to be identified as the author of Humpty Dumpty at Sea and Jan Lewis as the illustrator of this Work have been asserted in accordance with the Copyright, Designs and Patents Act, 1988.

ISBN 978 0 7496 8032 9 (hbk)
ISBN 978 0 7496 8038 1 (pbk)

Series Editor: Jackie Hamley
Series Advisor: Dr Hilary Minns
Series Designer: Peter Scoulding

Printed in China

Franklin Watts is a division of Hachette Children's Books an Hachette Livre UK company.
www.hachettelivre.co.uk

Humpty Dumpty

Retold by Brian Moses

Illustrated by Jan Lewis

FRANKLIN WATTS
LONDON•SYDNEY

Jan Lewis

"What am I painting?
Is it a ball?
It's that egg,
Humpty Dumpty,
falling down from
the wall!"

Humpty Dumpty
sat on a wall.

Humpty Dumpty had a great fall.

All the King's horses
and all the King's
men ...

... couldn't put Humpty
together again!

Humpty Dumpty

Humpty Dumpty

sat on a wall.

Humpty Dumpty

had a great fall.

All the King's horses

and all the King's men ...

 ... couldn't put Humpty

together again!

 Can you point to the
rhyming words?

Humpty Dumpty
at Sea

by Brian Moses
Illustrated by Jan Lewis

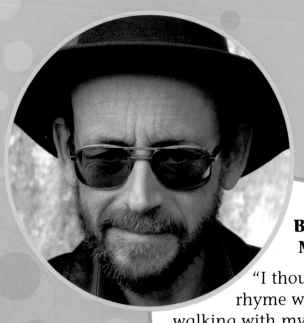

Brian Moses

"I thought of this rhyme while I was walking with my dog. She had just been swimming, and I suddenly pictured Humpty Dumpty in the water!"

Humpty Dumpty
fell off a rock.

Humpty Dumpty
had a great shock.

All the Queen's captains
and all the Queen's
crew ...

19

21

Humpty Dumpty at Sea

Humpty Dumpty
fell off a rock.
Humpty Dumpty
had a great shock.
All the Queen's captains
and all the Queen's crew ...
... tried to stick Humpty
together with glue!

Can you point to the
rhyming words?

Puzzle Time!

Which of these things might you take to the seaside?

Answers